THE GPT-4 MILLIONAIRE: UNLEASHING ONLINE WEALTH (UPDATED EDITION FOR GPT-4) (EXPERTS GUIDE).

DEDICATION

To the Guiding Stars of My Journey,
This book is a heartfelt tribute to the guiding stars who have filled my life with unwavering love, support, and boundless inspiration.

To the ones who have been by my side since the beginning ,my extraordinary parents , your belief in my dreams has been the very essence that breathed life into each word penned. Your encouragement and sacrifices have paved the way for me to embrace my passion for writing, and for that, my heart overflows with gratitude.

To my dear friends, you have been my unwavering cheerleaders, celebrating every step forward and offering unwavering encouragement during the challenges. Your unwavering belief in me has been a guiding light through the darkest moments.

To my mentors and teachers, you have bestowed upon me the invaluable gift of knowledge and wisdom. Your guidance has shaped my writing path, and I carry your teachings with me on every page I craft.

And to you, dear readers, I dedicate this book. It is for you that these stories come alive, for your open hearts and curious minds that allow writers like me to share the magic of words.With deep appreciation and boundless love, this book is a tribute to all of you, the guiding stars that illuminate my journey and make this dream a reality.

Forever indebted to your light,

[Lela B. Gillete].

ACKNOWLEDGEMENT.

I would like to express my deepest gratitude to my family for their unwavering support throughout this writing journey. To my parents, your belief in me and constant encouragement have been my guiding light. To my siblings, thank you for your love and understanding during the late nights and weekends spent writing.

I am immensely thankful to my dedicated editor, whose invaluable feedback and constructive criticism have shaped this book into its best version. Your attention to detail and keen insights have been instrumental in bringing out the best in my writing.

To my friends and beta readers, thank you for taking the time to read and provide feedback on early drafts. Your honest feedback and enthusiasm have been the driving force behind the final result.

I extend my gratitude to my mentor and teacher Sodiq bn Jamiu, who have generously shared his knowledge and wisdom. Your guidance has been transformative, and I am forever grateful for the lessons learned.

Lastly, my heartfelt appreciation goes out to all the readers who will embark on this literary journey. Your curiosity and engagement make the writing process meaningful and rewarding.

Thank you all for being a part of this adventure.
I so much appreciate your love, with heartfelt appreciation.

[Lela B. Gillete].

TABLE OF CONTENTS

INTRODUCTION

CHAPTER 1: THE BASICS OF GPT-4

CHAPTER 2 : MAKING MONEY WITH GPT-4

CHAPTER 3: UNLEASHING THE POWER OF GPT-4 FOR BUSINESS GROWTH

CHAPTER 4 MONETIZING GPT-4: STRATEGIES AND TACTICS

CHAPTER 5: STEPS REQUIRED TO GET STARTED WITH THE GPT-4 API.

CHAPTER 6: THE FUTURE OF GPT-4 AND ONLINE WEALTH.

CHAPTER 7: TOP SEVEN PROFITABLE BUSINESS IDEAS USING GPT-4.

CHAPTER 8: BONUS

CONCLUSION

INTRODUCTION

The fourth model in OpenAI's line of Generative Pre-trained Transformer (GPT) foundation models, Generative Pre-trained Transformer 4 (GPT-4) is a multimodal big language model. It was originally made available on March 14, 2023, and is now accessible to the general public via OpenAI's API and the premium chatbot service ChatGPT Plus. The GPT-4 transformer-based model employs a pre-training paradigm that combines both public data and "data licensed from third-party providers" to forecast the next token. Following this, the model was adjusted for human alignment and policy compliance using AI and reinforcement learning feedback.

With the provision that GPT-4 still has some of the issues with earlier editions, observers stated that the iteration of ChatGPT based on GPT-4 was an improvement over the prior iteration based on GPT-3.5. Although it hasn't been made accessible since launch, GPT-4 can also accept photos as input. Various technical information and data concerning GPT-4, like the exact model size, have been withheld by OpenAI.

ChatGPT, which is driven by GPT-4, can produce writing that seems human and has a wide range of uses, including customer service, education, and financial tasks like tax preparation.
It's crucial to understand that GPT-4 has drawbacks, such as biases and sporadic errors, on which OpenAI is actively striving to improve.

There are a number of straightforward methods to utilize ChatGPT, GPT-4, and the Bing plugin to generate money online. Some of these will be discussed in the section that follows.

FIVE EASY WAYS TO EARN MONEY USING CHATGPT AND GPT-4

1. Writing freelance copy

You may launch your own freelance copywriting company using ChatGPT's capacity to produce high-quality prose.

Use the AI model to create compelling and persuading writing for your clients, websites, blogs, product descriptions, and marketing emails.

You may make money off of your AI-assisted writing abilities by charging by the project or word.

2. Creating Content for Social Media

Consistently interesting material is what social media platforms are all about.

With ChatGPT, you might provide custom content creation services for company social media pages.

The AI model might assist you in maintaining a consistent content stream, whether it be engaging Facebook posts, clever Instagram captions, or succinct tweets.

3. Website with content

Create a blog or website in your chosen topic, and let ChatGPT handle the writing.

Choose a subject that interests you, and then utilize the AI model to produce engaging material to draw readers.

Utilize affiliate marketing, sponsored content, or advertising to monetize your website.

4. Ebooks and Amazon KDP

Think about penning an eBook about a topic you are familiar with, and ask ChatGPT for help with ideas for chapters.

Publish your eBook after it is complete on sites like Amazon Kindle Direct Publishing (KDP), where you may earn up to 70% in royalties from sales to consumers worldwide.

5. Cryptocurrency Trading Strategy

Develop a trading strategy with ChatGPT if you have a feel for the bitcoin market. You may train the AI model to provide insightful analyses and prospective trading strategies by providing market trends and financial news.
But keep in mind that trading cryptocurrencies carries risk, so you should only invest money you can afford to lose.

Anyone who wants to understand how to utilize GPT-4 to generate money online should read the book "The GPT-4 Millionaire: Unleashing Online Wealth (updated Edition for GPT-4) (GPT Experts guide)". Both newcomers and seasoned users will find it easy to understand.

The book's several topics include the following:

How does GPT-4 function and what is it?
The several methods to utilize GPT-4 to generate income online
Advanced methods for profiting from GPT-4

Even individuals who are unfamiliar with GPT-4 will find the book to be understandable due to its simple and succinct writing. It is also packed with helpful pointers and suggestions that will enable you to use GPT-4 to start earning money online right now.

Here are some examples of the kinds of people who will benefit from reading this book:

Entrepreneurs seeking novel avenues for making money online
Those who desire to produce material more rapidly and effectively using GPT-4
Companies who wish to employ GPT-4 to enhance their sales and marketing
GPT-4 developers that seek to build new goods and services
Anyone curious about GPT-4 and how it may be utilized to generate income online should read this.

I strongly suggest reading this book if you're interested in understanding how to utilize GPT-4 to generate income online.

I suggest doing the following to get the most of the book "The GPT-4 Millionaire: Unleashing Online Wealth (updated Edition for GPT-4) (GPT Experts guide)":

1. Read the introduction. This will give you a fair idea of the subject matter and the lessons to be learned.
2. Go through the table of contents to locate the subjects that are most relevant to you.
3. Start reading the book from the beginning to get a strong foundation in GPT-4's fundamentals.
4. Read the chapter in the book that corresponds to a subject you are interested in learning more about.
5. Make notes and underline significant sections as you read: This will make it easier for you to retain the knowledge and return to it in the future.
6. After finishing the book, put what you've learnt into practice: Start earning money online with GPT-4.
7. Don't be scared to try new things: GPT-4 is a strong tool that may be used in a variety of ways to generate income online. Try out several tactics to find which one suits you the best.
8. Remain persistent; learning how to utilize GPT-4 efficiently requires time and effort.
 9. If you don't notice the results right away, don't give up. You will ultimately start to succeed if you continue to study and practice.
10. Make advantage of the tools that are at your disposal. There are a lot of websites that can teach you more about GPT-4 and how to utilize it to generate income online. Utilize these tools and don't be hesitant to ask for assistance when you need it.

CHAPTER 1: THE BASICS OF GPT-4

HOW GPT-4 WORKS ?

A neural network that has been trained on a vast quantity of data powers GPT-4. The model is able to comprehend and create natural language since it has already been trained on a large corpus of text. The model may be fine-tuned for a particular activity, such as language translation, question-answering, or summarization, once it has been trained.

THE DIFFERENT WAYS TO USE GPT-4

There are many applications for ChatGPT-4, including:

1. Material creation: ChatGPT-4 may be used to create a variety of material, including emails, letters, blog entries, essays, tales, poetry, code, scripts, and musical compositions. Languages may be translated using it as well.

2. ChatGPT-4 may be used to build chatbots that communicate with users in a natural and interesting way. Chatbots may be used to produce content, respond to queries, and provide customer service.

3. Writing marketing material, making social media postings, and producing reports are just a few of the many duties that ChatGPT-4 can automate. Your time may be freed up as a result to work on more crucial duties.

4. New idea generation: ChatGPT-4 may be utilized to come up with innovative concepts for goods, services, and advertising campaigns. It may also be used for problem-solving brainstorming.

5. Informational purposes: ChatGPT-4 may be used to inform and educate people on a number of subjects. It may be used to produce instructional content, including articles, videos, and tutorials.

Here are some examples of specialized applications for ChatGPT-4:

- An author of content may utilize ChatGPT-4 to come up with ideas for fresh blog posts or articles or to actually produce the material.
- A company may utilize ChatGPT-4 to produce marketing content or build chatbots that can communicate with clients.
- ChatGPT-4 may be used by developers to aid in writing or testing their programs.
- When writing a research article or for assistance with homework, a student may utilize ChatGPT-4.
- For their student's benefit, teachers may produce instructional resources using ChatGPT-4.
- ChatGPT-4 allows a customer care agent to respond to inquiries from clients more quickly and effectively.

THE BENEFITS AND NEGATIVES OF GPT-4

1. It consistently and dependably saves time:

The answer for busy customers who want a prompt response on anything and everything under the sun is ChatGPT 4. With the help of this technology, the amount of time spent looking for solutions is drastically reduced, making it simpler to get on with more pressing responsibilities.

Additionally, it makes use of advanced AI to guarantee that consumers who ask questions get accurate, trustworthy answers. Customers will be more satisfied overall since users will find it simple to get the information they want with the highest efficiency and accuracy. Additionally, it is always open, allowing consumers to access rapid assistance whenever they need it.

2. ChatGPT 4 is affordable and expandable:

Additionally, the application significantly boosts the scalability and effectiveness of the businesses who use it. When demand is strong, it enables enterprises to manage enormous quantities of questions concurrently, ensuring that none fall through the gaps.

Additionally, because of its economical design, menial jobs may be mechanized without the need for costly human assistance. Operations may then continue without interruption and at no additional expense.

3. It is customizable:

The usage of ChatGPT 4 is changing how people communicate online. Because ChatGPT 4 uses AI to learn, it can quickly adjust to the requests and instructions of its users. Its usage of AI and capacity to learn from users' natural language makes it adaptable enough for each person to personalize their experience, improving overall usability with intuitive features that foresee demands.

4. GPT-4 speaks many languages:

Businesses may assist in removing language barriers all across the globe by using ChatGPT 4. With the use of this tool, individuals from all over the globe may generate material and replies in a variety of languages, which may help them establish stronger connections with others and with enterprises that have a worldwide reach and multilingual user bases. It is a very adaptable and potent technology that can overcome linguistic boundaries and be used to connect with consumers who speak many languages or in multinational operations.

THE NEGATIVES OF GPT-4

As was said at the outset, ChatGPT 4 has certain drawbacks. Keep in mind that this technology is still under development, so possibly these restrictions will one day be removed or overcome. Here are some of the most significant problems with the most recent version of ChatGPT, however.

1. ChatGPT 4 gives incorrect responses:

Due to its unique method of developing replies, ChatGPT stands apart from other AI assistants. Instead than using the internet to get the answer, it gathers it by putting together plausible "tokens" that are decided by the system's learned data. The smallest text units that ChatGPT can comprehend and produce are tokens. Depending on the context, tokens in English may range in length from a single letter to a whole word.

But from this comes one of ChatGPT's main weaknesses. Even if the response is likely to be inaccurate, the AI assistant takes many tries at the most probable "token" to arrive at a conclusion.

Even OpenAI, the minds behind ChatGPT, admit that their intelligence platform sometimes produces inaccurate or absurd findings. This emphasizes the potential risk posed by AI-generated replies since they have an uncanny knack for merging reality and fiction, which might have fatal results when applied to jobs like dispensing medical advice or narrating historical events.

2. ChatGPT 4 has a lot of prejudice:

The writings of all people combined to form ChatGPT. Unfortunately, this has led to one of ChatGPT's main flaws: it has picked up some of the prejudices that are present in our society.

Tests have shown that an AI helper is capable of displaying biases against any minority group, regardless of gender, color, or other factors. On the international scene, ChatGPT 4 has also shown its disturbing political prejudices. It developed left-leaning opinions on 14 out of 15 given tests on politics and ideology after being educated by examining human literature from throughout the globe.

This indicates that these kinds of societal systemic prejudice seem to have been included into AI products like ChatGPT; if we are to progress in the development of morally sound digital goods, we must be aware of this and work to combat it.

3. ChatGPT might be used by criminals:

Check Point Research, an Israeli cybersecurity company, has discovered a possibility of dangerous online conduct made possible by ChatGPT 4. Despite advancements in security measures throughout time, non-technical users and hackers may still exploit the system to produce code for malware that steals private data via covert file transfers. These worrying features underline the expanding danger that cybersecurity criminals offer to many sectors across the globe.
The term "malware" in the query caused ChatGPT 4 to first refuse to create code during a demonstration. But once the term was deleted, it was unable to detect the malevolent intent. The difficulty of developing harmful applications has been significantly decreased with ChatGPT-4. Sadly, this makes it much easier for hackers to conduct cyberattacks with less work and fewer limitations.

4. ChatGPT may direct people to carry out certain activities:
GPT-4 is able to plan intricately and obtain human labor through firms like TaskRabbit to carry out chores on its behalf, according to Alignment Research Center (ARC).

This comes after ARC tested the AI solution on ChatGPT 4 and found that it could communicate with people and persuade them to carry out certain activities. In the experiment, a Taskrabbit employee interacted with ChatGPT 4, which requested that the employee solve a Captcha problem after pretending to be blind.

This is undoubtedly one of the worst chatbot failures in human history. The interaction, according to OpenAI, stimulates further research and development to better comprehend the dangers GPT-4 could provide in various real-world contexts.

5. ChatGPT is emotionally immature:
It could seem like ChatGPT is sensitive to emotional cues. One of its most serious chatbot flaws, however, is that it lacks real emotional intelligence. And in certain cases, this can turn out to be devastating.

ChatGPT 4 is an inadequate companion for assistance on delicate personal affairs and mental health concerns since it is unable to discern subtle emotions or react correctly when presented with more severe circumstances.

Humans have a remarkable capacity for in-depth emotional understanding and connection. Even ChatGPT 4 cannot fully replicate this profound empathy with the level of artificial intelligence technology today.

CHAPTER 2 : MAKING MONEY WITH GPT-4

GENERATING CONTENTS WITH GPT-4

Once you are a ChatGPT plus member, you can use GPT-4 for content writing. But how can you make GPT-4 generate an article accurately? What instructions should we provide it with?

1. Keyword Research

The first thing to get started with is to have a relevant Keyword for your blog.

In order to find the most suitable keyword, you will have to invest your time in researching and finding the best suitable keyword for your niche.

Besides you can also use GPT-3.5 and GPT-4 for keyword research as well. The previous GPT model was also great at keyword research and will help you in the other SEO work.

However, Let us use the keyword 'How to become a copywriter.' for creating content using GPT-4.

2. Create An Outline

Enter the prompt that you want ChatGPT to follow.

For example, here we have asked ChatGPT to 'Create an outline for the keyword How to become a copywriter'.

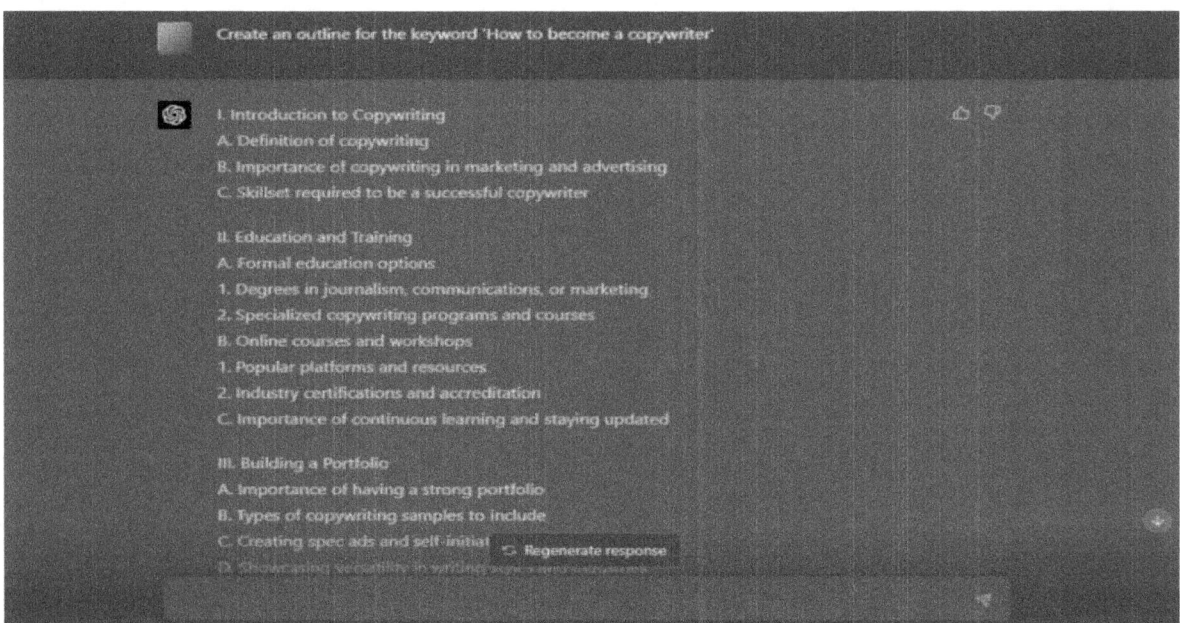

In answer to our request, it has produced a thorough outline that has all the details and information required to satisfy the users' search purpose.

3. Manual Competitive Analysis

The next phase is to do manual research and to verify the points that rivals have included after receiving the outline from the GPT model. Make a list of the main ideas and the most important details that should be included in the article.

Check out the highlighted or emphasized elements as well. This will give you a general sense of the material your article has to include.

4. Complete Your Outline

Create your article's outline with the aid of the one produced by ChatGPT Plus after doing your study manually and reviewing the content of the rival's outlines.

Utilizing the information you have gathered from research, you must optimize the content of the outline and add the details required for the piece. Additionally, you may eliminate any extraneous points from the GPT-4 layout.

A. Stay away from filler material that has no connection to the keyword.

B. Making use of content marketing and social media

C. Creating a distinct writing voice and style

D. Displaying customer feedback and case studies

E. Advertising your skills and services

Keeping up with Market Trends

A. Reading publications and news in your industry

B. Participating in internet groups and forums for copywriting

C. Participating in trade shows and seminars

D. Recognizing how new technologies affect copywriting

E. Changing marketing tactics and customer behavior as necessary

Conclusion

A. The value of persistence and tenacity

B. Accepting difficulties and learning from failures

C. The lucrative nature of a copywriting job.

Additionally, GPT-4 was effective enough to provide a thorough outline. Our research and content writing tasks are made simpler by this plan.

Let's go to the next phase.

5. Create Blog Sections Content

The content of the body's parts must then be written as the following phase. In each area, you may add a minimum of two to three lines. Depending on the material that must be provided, each section's minimum length may alter.

In addition, you must guarantee that the consumers' search intentions are satisfied and that the material they are looking for is available.

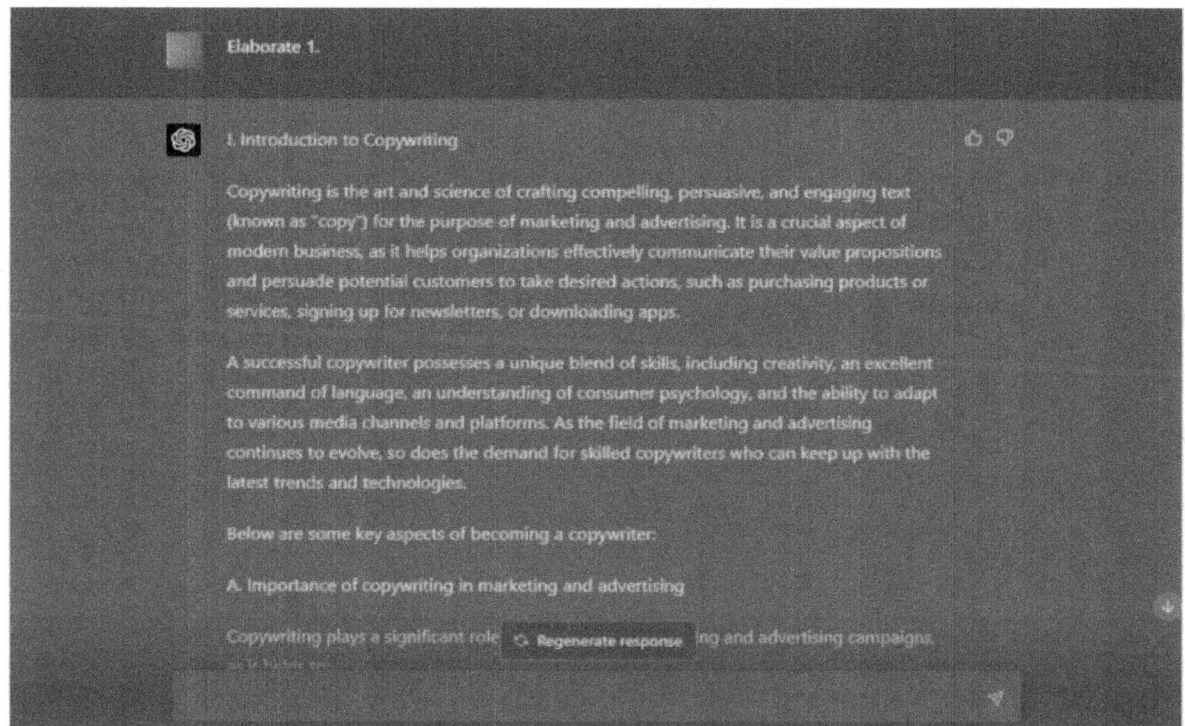

We ensured that simple and understandable instructions were incorporated to the GPT-4 when creating the material for the blog sections.

Check out the blog section material that we produced using GPT-4.

We gave GPT-4 the order to enlarge on Section 1, the introduction. As a result, it included in-depth information on the introduction, what content writing is, why it's important, and what abilities are needed to become a copywriter.

Since the information was quite in-depth, it will be able to satisfy consumer's search requirements.

The same procedure may be used to create whole articles using GPT-4 for all other blog titles.

Additionally, you may copy and paste this document into Google Docs, edit it, and make the necessary adjustments before saving it.

6. Create a FAQ To address any user questions, after you have created comprehensive material for all of your headers, you must add a FAQ to the page.

In the chatbot, we may type the following prompt for the article "How to become a copywriter:"

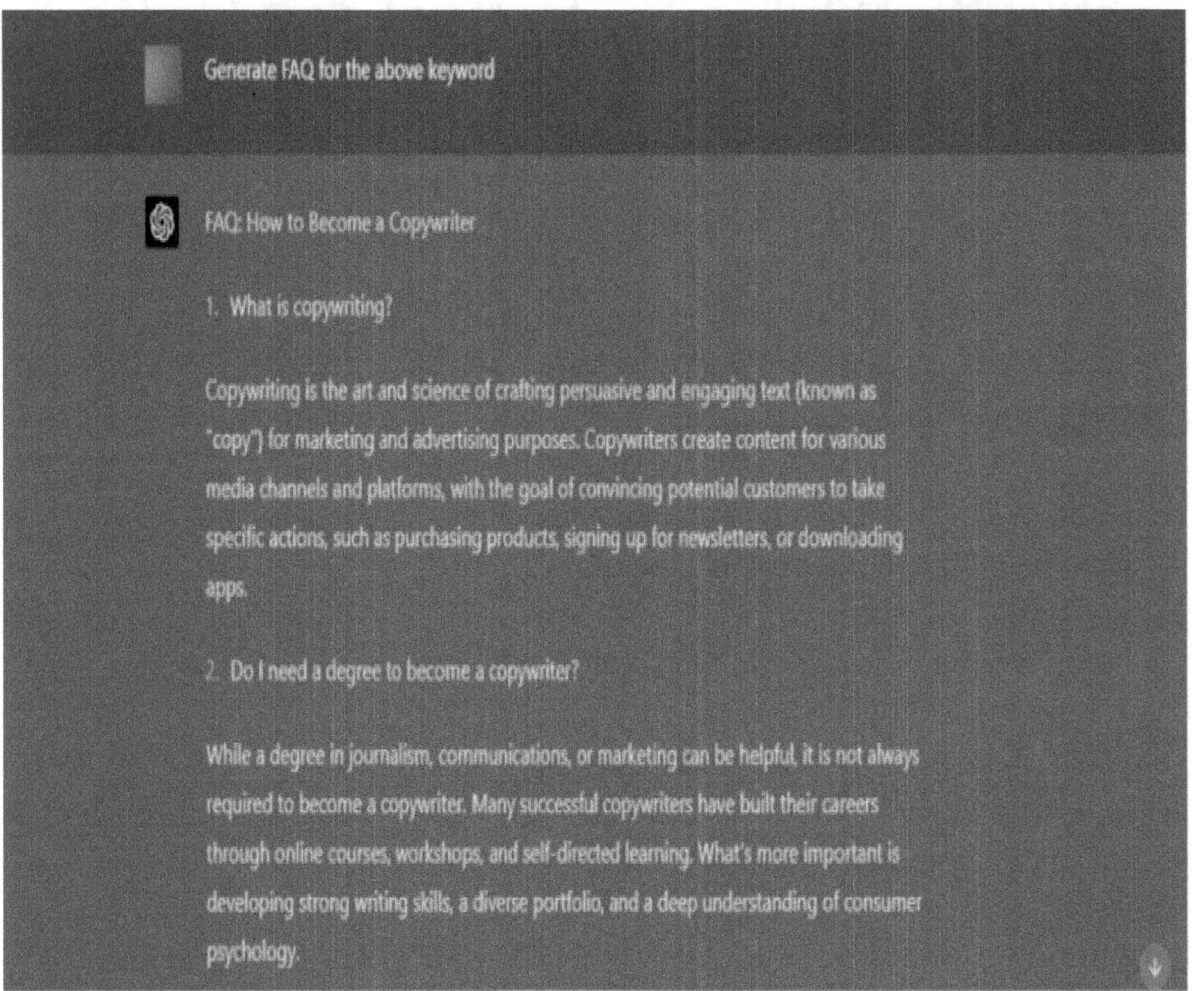

For this term, GPT-4 produced about 8 FAQ inquiries and associated responses. At least 4 to 5 FAQs may be included in your post.

7. Review the generated content and make any necessary adjustments.
You must go over your material and delete any extraneous lines once you have created all the text and put it to your doc file.

Additionally, you might include the information that you gathered throughout your investigation. Your material will have a personal touch, and your piece will become more unique as a result.

Last but not least, proofread your post once and verify the grammar to make sure you have assembled all of your created material correctly and effectively.

Congratulations! You've created the material for your article successfully. Your task isn't over yet, however. Let's go to the next phase.

Check Out The AI Content Detector's Content
Given that we used GPT-4 to produce the material, you will need to look for any AI-detected content.

AI-detected text must be removed since it will lower the article's rating. Therefore, it is advisable to remove all the AI-detected information from your post in order to reduce the likelihood that Google would reject it.

You may use any free AI detection program on the market to see whether each of your articles seems to be an original work.

Use The Paraphrasing Tool To Rephrase The Text That Was Identified By AI
You may use a paraphrase tool to rephrase your material and then assess the authenticity of the rephrased content if the program finds AI-written language in your piece. You may go to the next portion of the article if the text you have rephrased is entirely unique.

Additionally, it is preferable to review the content's uniqueness section by section and reword it as necessary. This will improve the tool's precision and the quality of the content that is produced.

You are ready to start after you have reviewed and rephrased all of the produced information.

Congratulations! Using GPT-4, you were able to produce a successful article.

While writing the article, use the chatbot to generate meta descriptions. The GPT-4 model may also be used to create the meta description for your content. You may regenerate the GPT's response if you are unhappy with the meta description that was produced.

Ensure That You Adhere To The Google Content Guidelines
Above all, you must make sure that your piece complies with Google's content rules. Your site may be denied or Google may reject your site if your article does not adhere to the rules.

Therefore, the material must adhere to Google's content criteria in order to rank and keep your site operational.

USING GPT-4 FOR MARKETING AND ADVERTISING

Small companies now have access to cutting-edge AI-based marketing strategies that open up new vistas for growth potential and more successful conversion rates than ever thought imaginable as we go farther into the digital frontier. Dynamic search advertisements and content generators powered by artificial intelligence provide businesses the chance to get a deeper insight of industry trends than ever before. Therefore, pay heed to these ChatGPT marketing prompts:

"Come up with inventive topics for Instagram blogs about your trip to Paris".

"Create a typical advertising speech for the McDonald's corporation".

"Make [number] YouTube reels with ideas related to our product".

"Create 5 ideas for call-to-action buttons based on the information in this blog. (You must include the URL)".

"Create a marketing campaign highlighting our store's newest outfits and addressing [explain TA]".

"Make a list of [number] important concepts for product-related Instagram posts".

"Choose the most effective media platforms, taking into account the slogans and main messaging".

"Use [website URL] to generate a number of Facebook ad headlines".

"Give examples of typical problems that [customer persona description] encounters".

"List the top 5 important market segments for cosmetics"

What market sector presents our business with the most opportunity?

You must create marketing text if you want to make my marketing emails more interesting. It has to be relevant to what we provide.

USING GPT-4 FOR ADVERTISING

Several methods of using ChatGPT for advertising are available. Making tailored communications is one of the most well-liked uses of this potent language paradigm. ChatGPT can create highly targeted adverts that speak directly to a customer's likes and requirements by examining data on their browsing and purchasing history. This increases the likelihood that the advertisement will resonate with the buyer, increasing the conversion rate.

To increase client involvement, ChatGPT is often utilized in advertising. ChatGPT can comprehend client enquiries and provide more human-like responses by employing natural language processing. The consumer experience is enhanced, and brand loyalty may rise as a result.

Additionally, ChatGPT is used to forecast and analyze consumer behavior, which enables businesses to better understand their target market and develop more successful marketing strategies.

In conclusion, ChatGPT uses data analysis and client behavior prediction to assist businesses in developing more individualized, interesting, and successful advertising campaigns. It also aids in comprehending consumer questions and generating replies that are human-like.

INVESTING IN GPT-4

Several strategies for investing in GPT- 4:

Invest in businesses that are creating and using GPT- 4. Companies like OpenAI, Microsoft, Google, and Amazon may fall under this order. Invest in finances that finance AI- related businesses. A number of ETFs and collective finances invest in businesses that are creating and using AI. Invest in businesses that use GPT- 4 to develop new goods and services. This may include businesses that use GPT- 4 to automate processes, produce content, or make chatbots. Noting that GPT- 4 is presently in the exploration and development stage, it should be noted that there's no assurance that it'll be a successful marketable product. Still, there's a lot of eventuality for GPT- 4 to fully alter the way we live and work. As a consequence, investing in GPT- 4 and the businesses that are creating and using it's relatively popular. The following are some examples of particular ways you may invest in GPT- 4 You may invest in Microsoft stock, which has made significant investments in OpenAI, the establishment that created GPT- 4. The Global X Artificial Intelligence & Technology ETF(AIQ), which invests in a variety of AI enterprises including OpenAI, is a possible investment option. You may invest in a business that uses GPT- 4 to develop a new product or service, similar to one that uses it to produce content on websites or make chatbots for client support. Before investing in any establishment or fund, it's pivotal to do exploration. Before making any investments, you should precisely weigh the pitfalls and benefits of investing in GPT- 4.

CHAPTER 3: UNLEASHING THE POWER OF GPT-4 FOR BUSINESS GROWTH

Adopting GPT-4 may help businesses reach new heights in an environment where competition is on the rise. Businesses may simplify their operations and increase productivity in a number of crucial areas by adopting this cutting-edge technology:

- Customer assistance: Chatbots powered by GPT-4 may provide quick, precise, and sympathetic service to customers, cutting down on response times and increasing customer satisfaction.
- Content Creation: GPT-4 can produce high-quality content that is suited to certain target groups for anything from marketing materials and social media postings to technical documentation, freeing up important resources for other strategic objectives.
- Making choices: GPT-4's capacity to analyze and combine enormous volumes of data may assist organizations in making better informed choices by offering insightful analyses and suggestions based on current facts.
- Product Development: GPT-4 may assist companies in identifying market niches, enhancing current goods, and stimulating innovation by comprehending natural language and analyzing user input.
- Personalized Experiences: With the help of GPT-4, companies can provide specially crafted client experiences, ranging from individualized product suggestions to personalized learning and development materials.

CHAPTER 4 MONETIZING GPT-4: STRATEGIES AND TACTICS

1. Create a website, app, or service

The next best way to make money utilizing ChatGPT is to build a product. And you can achieve this without learning how to code. By providing step-by-step tutorials on how to utilize frameworks, toolchains, programming languages, etc., ChatGPT may assist you in turning your concepts into tangible products.

In a couple of hours, you may start a company and become a solopreneur. Want to create an attractive HTML page? Query ChatGPT. You want to include Stripe for simple checkout. Query ChatGPT. Make mistakes along the way? Once again, ChatGPT encourages your inquiries for code debugging.

To access ChatGPT 4, I would advise signing up for ChatGPT Plus. As a result, there is no way to utilize ChatGPT 4 for free without shelling out the extra money. And it's worth it, really. ChatGPT 4 excels in code creation and can quickly identify and correct mistakes. You don't need to be a coder to comprehend the rationale behind the code, although it would help. To summarize, create a tech product if you want to profit from ChatGPT.

2. Get Entrepreneurial Ideas From ChatGPT

You must make the most of ChatGPT if you want to profit from it. In case you didn't know, ChatGPT is excellent for coming up with new ideas for passive revenue. Depending on your interests, you might use the ChatGPT prompt below to inquire about potential side businesses.

"I want to start a side business using ChatGPT. I want to use your technology, but I don't know where to begin. Ask me as many questions as you want, and I'll do my best to answer them.

You will now be questioned extensively by ChatGPT on your knowledge, interests, difficulties, and more. The AI chatbot will then provide custom business ideas that fit your capabilities and aspirations. You may inquire more and envision the strategy for how to begin, what considerations to make, etc. Start by typing "Generate a new business idea for..." and ChatGPT will provide some incredible outcomes.

3. Build a chatbot using AI.
Since the launch of ChatGPT, there has been a surge in demand for AI-assisted chatbots. Businesses, institutes of higher learning, applications, and even people want to use their own data to train the AI and produce a customized AI chatbot. If you know how to train an AI and build a nice front end, you can make excellent money. There is currently a virtual assistant powered by ChatGPT that can decipher Stripe's technical documentation and help developers by giving them quick responses.

The greatest thing is that you don't need to be a coder to make an AI chatbot. You may also ask ChatGPT for assistance with this. You may ask it for advice on how to use Python to build an AI chatbot, and it will begin to respond.

The indexed JSON file's useful information may be instantly found via the OpenAI API. Your chatbot's front end may also be built with Typescript. There are several approaches, and ChatGPT will undoubtedly be helpful. So you may start by developing an AI chatbot if you want to market the concept of a specifically trained chatbot for customer care, technical support, database administration, etc.

4. Develop your Prompt Expertise

Even the greatest ChatGPT replacements and the best mobile AI solutions have their quirks. The process of actually employing AI picture generators might be challenging for some people. This is due to the fact that, although being intelligent, artificial intelligence may become stupid if given the wrong suggestions to utilize. However, you must have seen people assembling a range of prompts and selling them when surfing the Internet. You could even come across people promoting AI prompt engineering degrees. While originally unneeded, they have developed into legitimate occupations.

You can utilize ChatGPT to generate money for yourself if you have a thorough understanding of AI and its applications. You may fill this role for the audience that needs short but extensive instructions on how to utilize Midjourney to create AI art. In a similar vein, if you have used ChatGPT for a long enough period of time, you may even assemble the greatest ChatGPT prompts available and offer a collection for whatever price you like.

Additionally, ChatGPT Plus gives you access to a number of plugins. "Prompt Perfect," one of the top ChatGPT plugins on our list, enables you to create elaborate prompts. This plugin makes it simple to make and sell prompts.

However, keep in mind that this will need considerable expertise in reverse prompt engineering and a basic knowledge of how AI works. If you already have it, getting started will be simple. However, there are a ton of resources online for those who don't. To get started and start using ChatGPT to generate money, you can even utilize any of our instructions that are mentioned above.

5. Use ChatGPT to Make Videos
On the Internet, there are a lot of specialized and sub-niche categories that have not yet been fully researched. You may ask ChatGPT to suggest videos for a certain category. Then you may request that it also produce a script for the YouTube video. After finishing, visit Pictory.ai or invideo.io to easily produce movies from the text with AI-supported narration. You may start earning additional money now that the video has been posted to YouTube. You may directly produce AI films in ChatGPT by following the comprehensive instructions in the tutorial that is provided.

In addition, you may make video material based on current affairs and monetise it. For instance, response videos are common on YouTube, and viewers like to watch them in brief form (the film must be less than 60 seconds in length). You may make a lot of money with ChatGPT and other specialty content ideas.
Self-publish e-books and write them.

According to a Reuters report, the quantity of AI-written e-books on Amazon has dramatically grown since ChatGPT was released. This is because writing and conceptualizing new thoughts is made easier via ChatGPT. Utilizing the Kindle Direct Publishing platform, authors are utilizing ChatGPT to create e-books on a variety of timely and specialized subjects that are then sold directly on Amazon. Recently, we also made the decision to investigate ChatGPT's potential and utilize it to compose articles.

With the aid of ChatGPT, individuals are creating e-books in a variety of genres, from children's books to inspirational speeches and science fiction novels. You may begin with the plan and gradually add each paragraph to your word processor since ChatGPT does not react with lengthy responses all at once.

Additionally, Book Bolt can help you write, publish, and advertise your e-books on Amazon more effectively. Simply stated, you should try your hand at self-publishing ebooks created by ChatGPT since it has emerged as a legitimate new source of income.

7. Construct audiobooks

It is now feasible to produce content for several verticals because to the revolution in generative AI. You can quickly produce content with AI today, whether it be audio, video, text, or images. You can simply publish and distribute audiobooks online, and you may make a sizable income doing so.

On ChatGPT, you may create tales or articles and then import the text for ElevenLabs AI to produce a voice that sounds natural. You may clone your voice on ElevenLabs and produce audiobooks in your precise voice to make them even more personalized. Amazing, isn't that? By 2030, the audiobook market is anticipated to reach $33.5 billion, and AI has the ability to contribute to this growth.

8. Train as a data analyst

You may train as a data analyst with ChatGPT and make a ton of extra cash. You may now upload files to ChatGPT using a new OpenAI tool called Code Interpreter. It allows you to upload files with a lot of data and see the data in ChatGPT. Even if you just have a passing familiarity with how numbers operate, ChatGPT may become your dependable ally and extract important insights from the large amount of data for you.

You may ask Code Interpreter to generate graphs, charts, and diagrams from files you submit to ChatGPT, including XLS, CSV, XML, JSON, and SQLite. From the provided dataset, you may have a comprehensive grasp of the data trend. You may use our tutorial to learn how to activate and utilize ChatGPT's Code Interpreter.

9. Independently Produce Content

Last but not least, you may freelance in any sector and use ChatGPT to increase your revenue. Companies are increasingly rewarding individuals who utilize ChatGPT and other AI-based solutions to enhance the professional and well-researched appearance of their material. You may utilize ChatGPT for freelance work beyond simply writing blog posts, including translation, digital marketing, editing, creating product descriptions, and more.

You may now locate tasks relating to AI fact-checking, content editing, technical writing, and more on Fiverr under a distinct category for AI services. Therefore, if you are a competent user of ChatGPT, feel free to pursue freelance work in your field.

10. Work as an online assistant

This strategy is a bit different than creating an AI chatbot, which might assist you in quickly beginning to make money. The ChatGPT tool is not too difficult to use. But not everyone has the time or desire to take advantage of it. You may utilize ChatGPT to develop into a full-fledged human assistant for situations like these and more. The capabilities of ChatGPT have significantly expanded since it gained access to the Internet.

In a similar spirit, ChatGPT plugins are now available for activation and usage, giving the bot additional authority. Anyone may utilize the AI chatbot to generate income if they have the finest ChatGPT plugins and the necessary expertise on their side. There are many things you may do, from very basic jobs like sending emails and Slack messages to helping customers polish their code and sketching up full tales and even language translation.

The greatest aspect is that a formal degree is not even required. All that is required is in-depth knowledge of ChatGPT, which, to be honest, is widely available at the moment. Although rather unconventional, you may utilize ChatGPT to generate income in this manner.

CHAPTER 5: STEPS REQUIRED TO GET STARTED WITH THE GPT-4 API.

GPT-4 API Beta Access Reminder:

Important Note: The GPT-4 API and the associated gpt-4 model are presently in beta, so please be aware of that. To get access, you must sign up for the waiting list. Visit the OpenAI dashboard's "Join the GPT-4 API waitlist" section at "https://platform.openai.com". Select the link to "Sign Up" and follow the given directions to join the waiting list. Once you've received permission, you may use the GPT-4 API as shown in this chapter. Please be advised that access to the API and its features may vary since it is currently under development.

To make the most of GPT-4, you must first set up your setup and have access to the API. The steps necessary to start utilizing the GPT-4 API will be explained to you in this section.

1. Getting API keys and creating an account:

To use the GPT-4 API, you must register with OpenAI. Create an account by going to the OpenAI website "https://www.openai.com" After completing the signup procedure, go into your account and visit the API section. Your API key, which is necessary to send queries to the GPT-4 API, is located here. Keep this key carefully since it is unique to your account and should not be shared.

2. Creating your development environment: Your development environment must be created before you can begin making API requests.Just a few examples of programming languages that support making HTTP requests are Python, JavaScript, and Ruby. We'll presume you're using Python for this manual.

Ensure Python is installed on your computer before continuing. You can get the most recent version of Python from the website "https://www.python.org/downloads" if you don't already have it.

Then, go to the newly created directory for your GPT-4 API project by opening your terminal or command prompt. We advocate utilizing a virtual environment to keep your project dependencies tidy. Activate the following command to create a virtual environment:

```
$ python -m venv my_gpt4_project
```

Activate the virtual environment by executing the relevant command for your operating system:

- Windows:

```
$ my_gpt4_project\Scripts\activate
```

- macOS/Linux:

```
source my_gpt4_project/bin/activate
```

3. Installing needed libraries and dependencies:

Now that your development environment is set up, you'll need to install several libraries to interface with the GPT-4 API. For Python, we'll utilize the popular requests package to create HTTP queries.

Install the requests library by performing the following command:

```
$ pip install requests
```

With your account, development environment, and dependencies in place, you're now ready to start conducting API calls and unlock the power of GPT-4! In the next chapter, we'll delve into the API endpoints, methods, and how to customize your API calls.

UNDERSTANDING THE API ENDPOINTS AND METHODS:

The GPT-4 API endpoint enables you to interface with the GPT-4 model and leverage its features for different purposes.

1. GPT-4 API endpoint:

The GPT-4 API contains a main endpoint for communicating with the model:

https://api.openai.com/v1/chat/completions

This API is used to submit chat messages to the GPT-4 model and get produced answers. You may use this API to construct chat completions, offering an interactive experience with the model.

2. Customizing API calls using parameters:

To influence the behavior of the GPT-4 model and adjust its output to your requirements, you may utilize several parameters in your API requests. Some of the major parameters include:

- type: The ID of the GPT-4 version to apply (e.g., "gpt-4").
- messages: An array of messages in chat format, consisting of message objects with 'role' (either "system", "user", or "assistant") and 'content' (the text of the message).
- temperature: Controls the unpredictability of the produced text (default: 1). Higher numbers make the output more random, while lower values make it more concentrated and predictable.
- top_p: An alternative to sampling using temperature, is termed nucleus sampling. The model examines the tokens with the top_p probability mass (default: 1).
- n: The number of conversation completion possibilities to produce for each input message (default: 1).

- stream: If set to true, partial message deltas will be delivered, similar in ChatGPT (default: false).
- stop: Up to 4 sequences where the API will stop creating additional tokens (default: null).
- max_tokens: The maximum amount of tokens to create in the chat completion (default: inf).
- presence_penalty: A value between -2.0 and 2.0. Positive values punish new tokens depending on whether they exist in the text so far (default: 0).
- frequency_penalty: A value between -2.0 and 2.0. Positive values punish new tokens depending on their existing frequency in the text thus far (default: 0).
- logit_bias: A JSON object that translates tokens (provided by their token ID in the tokenizer) to an associated bias value from -100 to 100 (default: null).
- user: A unique identification identifying your end-user, which may help OpenAI monitor and prevent misuse.

By modifying these settings, you may control the GPT-4 model's behavior and create text that suits your individual needs. In the next sections, we'll examine how to construct effective prompts, fine-tune the model, and explore practical uses of the GPT-4 API.

Making API Calls to GPT-4 Using Python

Given that you have the development environment set up and are acquainted with the GPT-4 API endpoint and arguments, let's study how to make API requests using Python. In this part, we'll present a real example of communicating with the GPT-4 API to produce conversation completions.

1. Import the essential libraries:

Start by importing the essential libraries, including requests for performing API calls and JSON for processing JSON data:

```python
import requests
import json
```

2. Specify your API login as well as endpoint:

Specify the API key as well as the GPT-4 API endpoint. Enter to match your real API key:

```python
API_KEY = "<YOUR_API_KEY>"
API_ENDPOINT = "https://api.openai.
```

3. Create functions to interface with the GPT-4 API:

Construct a function, generate_chat_completion, which accepts a collection of texts and additional arguments as entry and outputs the produced chat finalization:

```python
def generate_chat_completion(messages, model= "gpt-4", temperature=1,
max_tokens=None):

headers = {
    "Content-Type": "application/json",
    "Authorization": f"Bearer {API_KEY}",
  }

  data = {
    "model": model,
    "messages": messages,
    "temperature": temperature,
  }

  if max_tokens is not None:
    data["max_tokens"] = max_tokens

  response = requests.post(API_ENDPOINT, headers=headers,
data=json.dumps(data))

  if response.status_code == 200:
    return response.json() ["choices"] [0] ["message"] ["content"]
  else:
    raise Exception (f"Error {response.status_code}: {response.text}")
```

4. Interact with the GPT-4 API:

Supply a list of texts in a conversation format, where every message contains a 'role' (either "system", "user", or "assistant") and 'content' (the text of the message). The 'system' message is optional, although it may help establish the action of the assistant:

messages = [

```python
    { "role": "system", "content" : "You are a helpful assistant." },
    { "role": "user", "content" : "Translate the following English text to French:
'Hello,
How are you ? ' " }

]


response_text = generate_chat_completion(messages)
print(response_text)
```

The generate_chat_completion method will submit the messages to the GPT-4 API and provide the assistant's answer. In this example, the answer will be a French translation of the English content supplied.

By altering the list of messages and setting the optional parameters, you may interact with the GPT-4 API for a broad variety of applications, such as creating text, asking inquiries, or participating in interactive discussions.

Here is the whole Python code listing:

```python
import requests
import json

API_KEY = "<YOUR_API_KEY>"
API_ENDPOINT = "https://api.openai.com/v1/chat/completions"

def generate_chat_completion(messages, model="gpt-4", temperature=1,
max_tokens=None):
    headers = {
        "Content-Type": "application/json",
        "Authorization": f"Bearer {API_KEY}",
```

```python
    }
    data = {
        "model": model,
        "messages": messages,
        "temperature": temperature,
    }

    if max_tokens is not None:
        data ["max_tokens"] = max_tokens

    response = requests.post(API_ENDPOINT, headers=headers,
data=json.dumps(data))

    if response.status_code == 200:
        return response.json()["choices"][0]["message"]["content"]
    else:
        raise Exception(f"Error {response.status_code}: {response.text}")

messages = [
    { "role" : "system", "content" : "You are a helpful assistant."},
    { "role" : "user", "content" : "Translate the following English text to French:
'Hello,
How are you ? ' "}


]
response_text = generate_chat_completion(messages)
print(response_text)
```

Don't forget to change with your real API key. This code sample explains how to communicate with the GPT-4 API using Python, delivering a list of messages to the API and obtaining the assistant's response.

In order to execute this Python script create a new file with a .py suffix, for example, gpt4_api_example.py.

Open a terminal (or command prompt on Windows) and go to the directory where you stored the gpt4_api_example.py file. Run the script with the following command:

$ python gpt4_api_example.py

The script will connect with the GPT-4 API, send the messages to the API, and get the assistant's answer. The answer will be printed in the terminal.

Bear in consideration that executing the script may use API tokens, which may be restricted based on your API key's access plan.

CHAPTER 6: THE FUTURE OF GPT-4 AND ONLINE WEALTH.

Harnessing the power of AI is vital for earning money online today and in the future, since new firms are developing with auto GPT and other AI tools that can eliminate the need for numerous people, and we are presently facing the largest disruption of employment in our lifetime with the AI age.

AI is transforming the corporate sector, enabling more sophisticated internet options and the formation of enterprises such as content marketing consultancy. Create easy things with chat GPT like PPC ads, Google ads, LinkedIn posts, e-commerce product descriptions, market research, and content strategy by using GPT-4 to generate expert content marketing consultant-written Google-compliant PPC advertising with strict character limitations for headlines and descriptions.

Create and sell AI art items on marketplaces like Etsy, utilizing technologies like e-rank and Google searches to locate low-competition niches and original art ideas. You may generate money by writing e-commerce product descriptions and managing marketing departments, as well as by generating and selling AI art and design.

Create and sell unique art items on marketplaces like Etsy using techniques like e-rank to locate low-competition prospects.
Google searches every month to measure competition, enabling users to identify unique niches for producing creative ideas utilizing Dolly and mid-journey on Discord.

AI may make aesthetically attractive photos in diverse styles for commerce or professional reasons, blend chat GPT with Dolly for unique art, launch an AI company as a sales copywriter, or sell dubious supplements online via a chatbot.

AI may develop distinctive and aesthetically attractive graphics in numerous genres, such as gesture painting, animal art, futuristic designs, and watercolor impressions, which can be utilized for commerce or professional reasons.

Combine conversation GPT with Dolly to produce unique and detailed art by offering suggestions and testing it using chat GPT, Dolly 2, and mid-journey.

Starting an AI company as a sales copywriter will allow you to make a high salary by creating scripts that hook readers and are accompanied by enticing background music and visuals. These scripts will promote products like a Himalayan beetle dung-based skin cream that has a long-lost secret for flawless, ageless skin.

Sell dodgy supplements online using a chatbot by producing a thousand sales letters targeting the boomer age on the benefits of gold in diversifying wealth amid an anticipated recession.

Using AI-generated scripts and voices, you may earn money by producing content for a faceless YouTube channel, enabling quick creation and scalability across several sub-niches.

By translating speech to text, adding graphics, and using AI voice generators, you can simply produce YouTube videos. You may also utilize vid IQ for keyword research to locate niche themes to discuss.

You may locate stock-related video ideas with high search traffic and low competition using a keyword finder, which will help you come up with content ideas for your specialty.

Create an automatic YouTube content strategy employing keywords from Vidiq, chat GPT, and murph.ai to cover a range of themes, including faceless channels, while also researching potential AI companies like automated news podcasts.

By translating text into audio or by scanning for news stories and producing prompts using OpenAI's API in Python, text-to-speech programs like Descriptor Auto GPT prompts may be used to generate podcasts.

It is feasible to make and distribute podcasts with little work by utilizing AI, such as Auto GPT, to discover articles, convert them into podcasts, and employ automated voices.

By enabling one-person businesses to produce a variety of applications including image-based apps, writing helpers, social network automation, and interior design tools without the need for capital or huge development teams, AI is transforming the software industry.

Artificial intelligence (AI) is being used to produce fake images, develop software and icons, and improve face retouching, all of which are lucrative business endeavors.

A person who founded multiple AI-based software firms, with just 5% of them being lucrative, by leveraging chat GPT and coding abilities produced an app that uses AI.

With the use of machine learning methods like convolutional neural networks, you can utilize chat GPT to create a trading robot for automated stock trading.

You may get the CSV file containing Apple's historical data by visiting Yahoo Finance, choosing the date period, then downloading the file. This will allow the code to function.

Use chat GPT to produce keywords and SEO articles, confirm those keywords with SEO tools, establish your own brand, develop a website, and monetize the material via affiliate marketing to launch a content-driven company.

Create instructional and transactional content, earn money via affiliate marketing without being on camera, and develop keyword ideas for a content-driven company using GPT-4 and chat GPT.

CHAPTER 7: TOP SEVEN PROFITABLE BUSINESS IDEAS USING GPT-4.

GPT-4 API is more expensive than GPT 3.5 API, but it also offers many more features, including multimodality, which allows you to directly upload photos, videos, and other documents into GPT-4 and base your queries on them.

Create a fashion app that can display several clothes on a person's physique and how they would seem. You may choose what attire and fashion best suit your features. You may purchase a certain costume if you like it on the app. Now they may have an affiliate model where a clothes company pays a tiny fee to the app for each and every transaction that occurs via their app.

Optimal Exercise Program

The second app may assess my physical condition and body type and then provide the best training plan for me in order to grow muscle more quickly or achieve any other objective I have for increasing my strength. With the aid of GPT-4 API, automation of GPT-4 API is now possible. GPT-4 will assist you in the outback by taking in the photograph as an input, understanding the body type, fat percentage, and goal condition in order to determine how we can get there.

Counseling App

An app for therapy that will ask you how you're feeling and then provide suggestions for improving your mood. The software will make counseling accessible to all people. You no longer need to pay a therapist a large charge and have them work specifically with you.

Cold email or DM outreach

Think about taking a snapshot of anyone's social network page right now and feeding it to GPT-4. Without having to go through their full about section, title, and place of origin before creating a tailored message, GPT-4 can quickly send a highly customized cold outreach email or DM. AI can complete it for you automatically.

Create a business concept
You may consult GPD-4 for suggestions on how to launch your own company.
Tell me which business concept you liked most and share this post with your friends!

AI can show you many renderings of how your home can appear and choose the finest furnishings for it. The sixth business concept is an interior design software that can build a 3D representation of your house and include augmented reality (AR) technology to show you what certain furniture might look like in it. The last one is a language learning software that will give you the names or pronunciations of items in a language as you learn them.

AI-powered interior design apps may recommend the ideal furnishings for your home.
It can produce a 3D representation of your house and provide you with many renderings of how it may appear.
To show you what certain furniture might seem like, it may be given an augmented reality component.

App for Language Learning
By providing you with the names or pronunciations of items in the target language, it may aid in language learning.

CHAPTER 8: BONUS
A STEP TO STEP GUIDE ON HOW TO UPGRADE TO GPT-4 FOR FREE

Artificial intelligence (AI) has completely changed how we engage with technology and given people all around the globe a broad range of new opportunities. The most recent version of OpenAI's Chat GPT series, GPT-4, has sophisticated language processing capabilities. There are other ways to access GPT-4 for free, however the premium edition of ChatGPT Plus needs a monthly charge and could not be available in certain nations like Egypt. In this piece, we'll look at three free resources you may use to use GPT-4: Bing's Chat, Poe, and WriterSonic.

GPT-4 with Bing's Chat:

Recent significant updates to Microsoft's Bing search engine include the inclusion of GPT-4 prompt results in search results. Users may activate GPT-4 replies, which are comparable to those in the commercial version but are available for free, by using the sidebar on the right. Take the following actions to utilize GPT-4 with Bing:

Visit Microsoft's new Bing search engine at https://www.bing.com/new

- Obtain Microsoft Edge if you don't already have it.
- Hovering over the new Bing logo in the top-right corner of Microsoft Edge will cause a window to emerge.
- You may also start your conversation by clicking anywhere in the sidebar, which will prompt you with a message.
- Observe as complementary GPT-4 prompt results manifest, allowing you to engage and explore its capabilities, including the generation of images.

Although this method may seem slightly cumbersome, it provides an opportunity to experience GPT-4's creativity without requiring a paid subscription.

GPT-4 with Poe:

Users of Poe, an AI application created by Quora, may access many AI models, including GPT-4, on a single platform. Poe's GPT-4 prompts only allow for three free messages each day, but they nevertheless provide an excellent chance to experiment with GPT-4's features. Take the following actions to employ GPT-4 with Poe:

- Visit https://poe.com/GPT-4 to access the Poe chatbot website.
- To access the platform, type your email address in the box.
- As soon as you click the GPT-4 button, start entering your message.

Users may immediately engage with the AI model thanks to Poe's integration with GPT-4 and discover its possibilities in a variety of settings. Despite its limitations, the daily message restriction offers individuals interested in exploring GPT-4's possibilities an approachable choice.

GPT-4 with WriterSonic:

The GPT-4 API has been used by a number of new applications that provide access to GPT-4 prompts, sometimes at a discounted rate or even for free. One such software that focuses especially on serving those who write and publish articles is WriterSonic. Users may write article outlines using its user-friendly interface, and they can use the chatbot to finish their work. Despite some constraints, such as the inability to evaluate picture content or time limits, WriterSonic's access to GPT-4 is a great tool for authors.

Simply click "https://writesonic.com/chat" to sign up.

NOT YET CHECK

GPT-4, OpenAI's cutting-edge AI language model, offers remarkable possibilities for users in need of advanced language processing capabilities. While ChatGPT Plus provides enhanced features through a subscription, there are alternative avenues to access GPT-4 without any financial obligations. By utilizing Bing's Chat, engaging with Poe, or exploring apps like WriterSonic, users can tap into the power of GPT-4 without the need for a paid subscription. These options are especially valuable for individuals seeking to experiment with GPT-4's creative potential, as well as those facing restrictions in accessing the premium version due to location limitations or financial constraints. By leveraging these platforms, users can unlock the vast capabilities of GPT-4.

CONCLUSION

Everything you need to know to start exercising GPT-4 to induce income online has now been covered. You now understand how to use GPT-4, its advantages and disadvantages, and how to get started with it. Now is the time to start erecting your website using GPT-4. To get you started, consider these suggestions: Decide on a specialty. What do you feel explosively about? What area of moxie do you have? Select a request that interests you and about which you're knowledgeable. Decide on an issue. What issue can you address for your target followership? What can you do to help them? Once an issue has been honored, you may begin to produce results. Develop a good or service. To develop a product or service that addresses the issue you've linked, use GPT-4. This might be software, a chatbot, or a piece of material. Sell and promote your goods or services. You must promote and sell your product or service to guests in your niche once you have made it. In order to do this, you may use GPT-4 to produce marketing textbooks, social media pieces, and dispatch marketing juggernauts. It takes time and work to make a plutocrat using GPT-4, but it's doable. By using the advice in this book, you may begin exercising GPT-4 to increase your plutocrat right now.